I0115365

INTIMACY

AND THE BLACK MAN

FACE TO FACE WITH THE TRUTH ABOUT BLACK MEN

INTIMACY AND THE BLACK MAN
FACE TO FACE WITH THE TRUTH ABOUT BLACK MEN

COPYRIGHT 1996 BY DONALD E. LAW ALL RIGHTS
RESERVED. THIS EDITION PUBLISHED BY D. E. LAW
PUBLISHING AND PRINTED IN THE UNITED STATES
OF AMERICA. NO PART OF THIS PUBLICATION MAY
BE REPRODUCED IN ANY MANNER WHATSOEVER
WITHOUT WRITTEN PERMISSION, EXCEPT FOR
BRIEF QUOTATION IN CRITICAL ARTICLES OF
REVIEW.

FOR INFORMATION ADDRESS:
DONALD E. LAW
D. E. Law Publishing
LOUISVILLE KY40218
donald.law@insightbb.com
or
easylaw@juno.com

ISBN 0-9641537-4-2

PRICE $10.00

ACKNOWLEDGMENTS
To God The Almighty
Our Director and Producer!

To my Mother Sylvia, what can I say, the most beautiful person in the world!

To my Father Curtis, again, what can I say, you are the greatest!

To my Sisters, Sheryl and Yvette, they don't make them like you anymore!

To Tim and Bernice Hatch, thank you for your open and candid thoughts, you've both been an inspirational experience.

To my life long friend Cathy Phelps, you have given me so much joy!

To Ms. Everne Dickson, The world is truly blessed with your love and kindness; above your head hovers the brightest **HALO** for you are indeed an Angel. Although you had no way of knowing, you met me during one of the darkest moments in my life. As I stood before you, I received such awesome power from your spirit, it literally **"charged my battery!"** As I walked away from your shop in tears, I honestly felt that there is someone out here in this crazy world that does care. Thank you for all that you have given me. We don't always know how little things make such a big difference! So special is the love I have for you.

To **ALL** I give my deepest love, gratitude, and respect!

DEDICATION

This book is dedicated to the following people for their unparalleled support and/or inspiration:

Ms. Saundra K. Almond, your genuine spirit and persona dug deep into my soul to prevail over the moments of self doubt. I truly thank God for the many blessings I have received and you are among them!

Mr. Ancil Babb, you brought me into a new life through your presence, I thank God for you!

Ms. Daralene Jackson, what can I say, you accepted me unconditionally, what a special feeling, Thanx and I love you.

Ms. Julia P. Horne and Ms. J. Williams, you put the fire under my behind that I needed, I will be forever grateful.

Rev. Larry Brayboy, your vision is so incredible, your support and inspiration have been a genuine **POWER PLANT!** You are awesome!

Finally, Ms. Letitia L. Law, words do not exist to truly express what I gained through our moments together. You gave me something that no human being will ever be able to take away! Your encouragement and contribution have been unequaled and were an absolute must, God knows exactly what we need. May God continue to Bless you. I love you so much, thanx for everything!

WITH ALL THE LOVE THAT I HAVE I TRULY THANK YOU ALL!

PART ONE

T H E   P R 0 B L E M

PART TWO

THE S0LUTIONS

A WORKSHOP APPROACH TO PREVENTING PROBLEMS

INTRODUCTION

!   Let's agree to disagree.

!   Don't kill the messenger. (That's Me!)

!   Know that ahead of us is a time for healing and growth.

!   Everything should be taken in a positive light.

WHAT THIS WRITING IS ABOUT IS TRUTH AND UNDERSTANDING. It is not about man bashing; it is not about woman bashing; it is not about fault finding or pointing fingers. It is **not** about gender superiority. I say this because I need it to be a foregone conclusion prior to you reading this material. I have spent long hours to find the truth and I am very much aware that some things cannot be left for someone else to assume what my intentions are. There is no attempt on the part of the author to make excuses for the way Black men sometimes treat Black women, however, there are some fundamental reasons why this does occur. Hopefully we are clear on this issue, for our past has been brutal and the time for us to make our move is now!

Why is it that Black men and Black women are engaged in a power struggle and seem to be more and more unhappy together? How is it that various ethnic groups can come from all over the world and reap the fruits of the American dream, while we as a people watch them pass us by? They move up the socioeconomic ladder and **enjoy living** in America, while we struggle to maintain an existence far less than what we deserve. It became very clear to me that the reason had nothing to do with intellectual superiority, but rather has more to do with the choices we make and a level of self-acceptance within the family structure. In-other-words, the family structure has order and security. Everyone in the family accepts their role and responsibility, and has pride in the role they play. The mother, the father, and the children all know what the rules are that they must follow in order for them to succeed. They all know what each other believes. This seems to be consistent with all of the cases I have examined. However, the Black woman, for the most part, has not been given the opportunity to fully understand her Black man with whom she has relations. Basically this is true, not because he has been or is dishonest, but because the Black man has not been taught that he need not be afraid of this thing called intimacy. It is suggested that there is a massive amount of fear that is subconsciously associated with being intimate, showing someone your true feelings and thoughts.

Whether I am right or wrong about the information I present will never become an issue with me and hopefully not with you either. This is not to point fingers or bash anyone, but it is to be used as a tool to build a foundation upon which you can begin to develop a deeper understanding, have more joy, and happiness in your life, or just find peace of mind. This is my goal and this is God's desire. I only hope that in your travels down your life's path you remember in the tough times I love you and I will always be in your corner.

I would like for you to know that I could have marketed this publication for the general population, but my purpose is to serve Black people first. Please forgive me if the use of Black people, Black man, Black woman, etc. is out of sync with the more acceptable modern reference of African American. It is only used because it is shorter and that is part of my basic format for bringing this to you. Keep it short and to the point so it can be read fast and you won't forget what's in the beginning of the book before you reach the last page. In addition, you will be able to put this information into practice faster, if you so choose.

Note: I have elected to make this publication as compact as notes taken from any course taken in school or book you may have read. As much as possible pointless and meaningless examples have been omitted, except when necessary for clarification. The only thing that is truly important is what you may be able to relate to your own life experiences that will assist you in achieving the relationship you desire. In addition, the language used will be of a down-home nature. There will be no attempt to throw a bunch of egghead sophisticated words at you that will take too much of your valuable time to break down. I honestly feel what we all need now is just a plain talk-in to. For now let me say that I sincerely hope that the information contained in this book will make each day, starting with today, a sweet, happy, and memorable one. May you find true intimacy and be as happy and prosperous as God intended for all of us to be.

Many thanks to you.

LUV YA

DONALD

CHAPTER 1:

A KEY TO UNLOCKING HIS EMOTIONAL DOORS

Why choose to write on this subject of intimacy and Black men? My concern is best expressed in terms of this Chinese Proverb which says, "if we don't change direction, we may end up where we're headed." The only group of people on the face of God's great earth that truly care **anything** about Black men is our beautiful Black Sisters, however, our behavior toward these precious women is basically unjust, unfair, and irresponsible by all reasonable standards. And in all fairness as I'm sure you'll see, it is a two-way street. Now bare in mind, there has not been a major push to focus on the positive attributes of being born a Black man. To be born a Black man to me, is the most gracious blessing a man can be given. I would not trade this for anything in the world. Likewise, I and many Brothers would not trade a Sister for anything in the world.

As I began to search for answers to questions regarding human behavior with respect to my own relationships it became painfully obvious to me that there was not an abundant supply of information available to African American men or women developed from an African American male's perspective. Bare in mind, this material crosses the gender line, and in many cases even crosses the color line (if the shoe fits wear it, if the shoe fits and it's not your shoe wear it anyway). Furthermore, this material to the best of my knowledge deals only with the rule rather than the exception. It has been said that "if you are not part of the solution, you are part of the problem." Together we can experience the power from the freedom of expression in a loving environment, while progressing to a higher level of existence. Simply because you are reviewing this material says you are searching for some understanding, you are reaching out, I truly hope what I will share will provide some serious insight and provoke some thought about how we value ourselves.

You and I are a fortunate people in that we come from strong and healthy forefathers. Thoroughbreds so to speak. Realize that all the weak and sickly died during the long journey on the slave ships. Only the strong and determined made it through slavery and never gave up hope: I could not have done it. We take so much for granted today in that we now have a little protection from such cruel and brutal treatment. I felt compelled to do this book from an experience that opened my eyes. I will never be the same.

Something **G R A N D** happened to me the other day, I felt a connection to our beautiful Black women and decided to bring some insight into the problem of the lack of intimacy between Black men and women. Without getting into all the details, my last relationship was on-again-off-again over a period of years as I worked a full-time job, but I would always come home and fix dinner for my lady (she loved my cooking). I washed my own clothes and sometimes washed and pressed some of hers; I washed dishes, cleaned the toilets, etc. Each day that I returned home from work, upon entering the parking lot, I would always be very happy when I turned the corner and saw her car; I'd say to myself **"oh good she's home."** For months, I would sit in the living room after dinner and watch her walk from the kitchen into the bedroom to play video games on her computer. I kept hoping that one day she would take the time to sit and talk with me. That day never came. I continuously asked her what was it that I may have done that obviously had her treating me so coldly. I wanted to know, I needed a clue as to what was going on. To that question she would not respond.

One day I happened to be home when The Oprah Winfrey Show came on and her guests that day were Patti LaBelle, Dionne Warwick, and Gladys Knight. They sang "SUPERWOMAN" and I mean they **SANG** SUPERWOMAN. Listening to these three African Angels' sweet voices brought tears to my eyes as all the pain that was so deep inside came pouring out. As they pumped their lungs to deliver the words to this song, I realized that "I" was carrying the load of this "SUPERWOMAN." The pain was so overwhelming. It is almost beyond words.

Reflecting on issues that come up from time-to-time, it dawned on me that many women across all lines have voiced their concerns about the lack of intimacy with the men in their lives. I feel deeply connected and must say, if what I felt was remotely close to what our Sisters are going through, IT MUST STOP, NOW!! Our Sisters are far too precious to live and/or exist in a state of such pain. I truly hope that this material will be a foundation on which you can create a friendship with the very spiritual, personal, and emotional communication that will deliver our lives at the highest level of peace and joy going into the days and years to come.

WHAT ABOUT INTIMACY AND THE BLACK MAN?

If you asked one hundred Black men what their definition of intimacy is, you would probably get at least seventy-five variations of what it means to men, anything from knowing when she has her period, to, it's the sounds she makes when she is making love. The problem is that only one out of that one hundred men would come close to what it means to women; their definition would not do the average woman any good emotionally. I know without question Black men are indeed capable of being intimate and existing in an intimate environment with Black women. Maybe, we should not expect to arrive at a point where one can say, "okay, now you're being intimate with me," but, we should expect to feel that special level of closeness and should work toward attracting this thing called intimacy into our relationships. It can be as easy or as difficult as we decide it is going to be in our minds, why decide that it is going to be difficult? Ideally, there should be absolute and unconditional respect extended and a real sense of what the preferences are of the other person, that is know what the other person likes and doesn't like and respect it unconditionally. It is a must.

Why is it that the lack of intimacy injects such pain into a relationship? This can best be explained by looking at a few fundamental dynamics of a relationship. One thing that is common to almost all relationships is that there is a certain amount of familiarity that is established during the period two people are getting to know each other. Secondly, as time goes on, feelings between a couple continue to grow. And as these feelings grow the desire becomes stronger and stronger to make the other person's life as comfortable as possible, to be there for them. However, there are many times that we may have something troubling us and we choose not to share it with the one we love. I submit to you that in a relationship where there exists love and caring, if one person has something that's troubling them, then the other one is aware that there is a problem. Now this strong desire to be there for someone you love turns into incredible pain and a feeling of helplessness because not only can you do nothing, but you do not have a clue as to where to begin searching for answers. As a result of not knowing where to begin, we typically start to blame ourselves. We lose our self-esteem thinking we are the problem. We begin to second guess ourselves accepting the fact that there must be something wrong with us. We read books with titles that do not make common sense let alone contain the information we need to solve the problem or at least understand it. (NOTE: We must be **very** careful about the information we allow to become a part of what we believe. We must be certain that those we choose to listen to, are qualified to have a position on the subject, i.e., a woman of European origin is not qualified to tell anyone how I as a Black man feel.)

There is a proverb that says, "happy people are never wicked." If this is true, then possibly it will help to explain why there are so many young Black men in imprisoned in America. They may have been reared to be very unhappy not that this was the intent of their parents or society, but this is what has happened.

It is my belief that a large number of the young Black men in our prisons today, at the time they became incarcerated, were in some kind of a relationship with a Black woman or were actively pursuing a relationship with a Black woman. I personally know such a woman. I'll call her Niki. Niki, is so very beautiful, she is absolutely stunning, she has a smile that could stop a freight train **COLD!** Her personality is really beyond words, she is beautiful in every aspect of what a true woman is and should be. Unfortunately, her man was incarcerated. Although she had problems of her own, she would always go to considerable lengths to help other people, so she was often exhausted. Because her husband was imprisoned, she had to travel across the state to visit him; I frequently would drive her car so she could rest and enjoy her visit as much as possible. Through this we became very good friends and she will always be someone very dear and special to me.

Often during the long drive across the state, I would look at her and wonder, "How could any man do anything that would take him away from a woman this beautiful, a woman this caring, this warm?" I thought to myself, "This makes less than no sense! Why in the world would a man be out running the streets, when he could be at home sharing loving moments with this woman?" What could be so awful that he would be afraid to go home? It's called **INTIMACY!**

Note: *Some definitions are being supplied for clarification. Particular words spark a unique meaning with different people. As issues and topics are addressed words that are defined are being used in the context given.*

Let's define intimacy for the purposes of this text.

INTIMACY: *Open* and *honest* communication on a very *personal and emotional level.* (Also see pages 11 and 12.)

Many men, but especially Black men, fear this thing called intimacy. I suspect it is viewed as a condition of weakness or at the very least is thought to question ones manhood, but this offers the only explanation I could find to answer many questions and begin to address and solve particular problems in Black relationships.

One major problem we face as Sisters and Brothers is our inability to effectively communicate. So let's define communication.

COMMUNICATION: *The process or method of transferring thoughts and/or feelings between two people in an understandable manner. Note: If two people just randomly pass words back and forth, yet fail to transmit their message to the other person, then for the purposes of this discussion, they have not communicated.*

As Black men and women we must first begin just simply talking to each other in a more respectful manner, this is the first step in establishing effective communication. DISRESPECT KILLS THE DESIRE TO ACHIEVE ANY LEVEL OF INTIMACY! We must learn to communicate both ways, men to women and women to men, with the primary goal being to strive for a deep level of understanding. We must develop understanding and acceptance or face extinction. Let's define the two concepts presented here, understanding and acceptance.

ACCEPTANCE: *A comfortable mental state of total receipt of a person, idea, circumstance, a situation, etc. that one cannot change or alter. Being able to live in a state where one is not mentally or emotionally affected by the way things are. i.e., If we don't agree on a particular subject or idea, then we just don't agree, that's it, period.*

UNDERSTANDING: *A level of consciousness that gives rise to a total and unconditional acceptance of the differences between two people. Is it possible to really understand a person or their point of view without applying your mental focus to find the true meaning that someone is trying to express? We need to be able to honestly say, "I relate to what you are saying," whether or not you agree with what is said or expressed.*

Just how important is communication in a relationship? Communication means change and growth. How much of what we have learned have we acquired through communication? Would we be alive if someone did not take the time to teach us how to take care of ourselves? How else would we know how to prepare ourselves for the future, to feed, clothe, and house ourselves? Assuming you agree with this premise, it seems only logical that everything we have learned has been through some form of communication. This is why, I strongly feel the Black man is on the verge of becoming extinct, unless he learns to communicate and be intimate with his Black Woman.

There should be no fear of the unknown. Being intimate with a Black woman is a completely liberating experience. The process of digging into the depths of one's true spirit, then releasing it in the form of sharing that spirit with someone you care deeply for, is the beginning of true living. The closer we approach our true spirit, the closer we get to finding our true purpose in life, the reason why we exist. Communication involves a focused effort to develop an understanding of the person you are dealing with and being able to accept them unconditionally.

NOTE: Probably one of the biggest factors in the inability of Black men to communicate or be intimate is the feeling that if they open themselves up emotionally or mentally, they may experience humiliation, shame, or loss of dignity. Our thoughts reveal who we really are. All feelings are generated by our thoughts. In order for a person to really know who you are, they must know what you think because it tells them how you feel. **SHARE YOUR THOUGHTS! JUST BE YOURSELF!**

In order to unlock the emotional doors of the Black man, we must first know what he believes. This is the basis for all that he will say and do, in-other-words, his behavioral patterns are developed based on what he believes. Everything he does or does not do is a product of what he believes. If he believes that he's a real dog, then he will behave accordingly. If he believes his life is not worth living, then in turn he will think the same of other's lives as well. Thus he will have no problem destroying his own mind and body and the minds and bodies of other people as well. And likewise, if he **feels** loved and respected, he will be able to respond and function in that environment. This must be established in the very early years of a male's life.

If the Black woman for whom he has intense feelings, can **accept** his beliefs as being true, then she has made great strides toward achieving intimacy. It is not being suggested that whatever he believes **is** true or correct, but that in his eyes this is the truth as far as his knowledge goes. No amount of verbal abuse will succeed in getting him to change what he believes. It is very important to know and understand that he feels what he believes in a very strong way. Just know it is possible for anyone to change what they believe if they change their thoughts.

At this point let's look at a more complex working definition of intimacy for the remainder of this text. Intimacy is very open and honest communication on a very personal and emotional level in a mental state that is:

1) without an overwhelming fear of rejection or ridicule

2)   rooted on a very strong foundation of self-security; you love, respect, and accept yourself regardless of what other people think about your position because it is just how you feel

3)   guilt free

4)   worry free

5)   bound in absolute trust in the other person

6)   with the ability to forgive at all times

This definition is not intended to be all-inclusive, but will provide a foundation for this text and upon which to build a relationship, or at the very least a reference point from which to begin.

WHAT IS A GOOD BLACK MAN? First, and for the sake of simplicity let's define manhood by the qualities of strength, character, and courage. Therefore, the qualities of a good Black man should be one that possesses a majority of the following qualities: A LEADER, responsible, caring, honest, respectful, and hopefully employed or in active pursuit. Note: Obviously there is the question of intimacy reflecting on the "manhood." Therefore to fear this thing called intimacy contradicts the definition of manhood. How can a man expect to live up to this image of being a man, yet does not have the courage to be intimate with his woman?

As a starting point, there are ten questions for you to answer. Please have complete answers for each question, even if your response is "who cares?" When you are finished reading this book, it may be helpful for you to review your answers to see if any of your answers or perceptions change.

1) Do you feel that Black men have any particular reason for not being able to **openly** and **honestly** communicate on an emotional level with ease?

2) What is the most important quality Black men look for in Black women?

3) What things can be done to stimulate a deeper level of intimate communication?

4) When you meet someone, what things are **not** important to you?

5) What is the most important quality a Black man should have?

6)   What are three things you think that Black men fear?

    1)

    2)

    3)

7)   What reasons do you have to continue to have confidence in Black men?

8)   What do Black men expect from Black women in a relationship?

9)   When you have problems in a relationship, where can you go for help and have absolute trust in the advice you receive?

10)   What are at least four things that must be done to have an intimate relationship?

    1)

2)

3)

4)

CHAPTER 2:

HOW DOES HE STACK UP TO WHAT HE SEES?

Our history as African slaves in the fields, suggest that we have roots that are very spiritual in nature. We are connected to a spiritual being that has brought us from the depths of sheer misery to where we are today. It took tremendous strength and courage to survive; subconsciously most Black men today believe that they simply could not or would not have made it. We may at times even feel inferior to our Brothers that came before us. Our inability to communicate with our women is but a sign that this is true. Somewhere between the conscious and subconscious state we are very aware that we are incredibly strong and it is this strength that restricts us in our ability to communicate with our Black women.

I think everyone knows that traditionally as male children growing up, showing emotion is not expected to be expressed without having a negative association connected. This type of behavior is usually met with scorn, shame, and humiliation for displaying such behavior. For men, this can be a very painful experience even at such an early age.

The recollections most Black men have from childhood do not include an abundance of role models expressing feelings or emotions, with the exception of rage and anger. Until recently, I have very few memories of Black men crying on television. How many young Black males have ever seen their father's cry? What about their brother? As an adult, how many times have we seen a Black man cry? Human beings often will flee an environment that will produce feelings of humiliation and/or considerable emotional discomfort. Can you recall a time when you left a particular situation because you deemed it too painful to handle? If so, make a note.

The images of strong Black men of the past are deeply rooted in the minds of every Black man alive, or at least they should be. Unfortunately, Dr. Martin Luther King Jr., Malcolm X, Marcus Garvey, and countless others of their caliber are seemingly so far removed from the image most Black men have of themselves; this image is constantly reinforced by way Black men are portrayed by the media. In addition, due to the exclusion of our true African history in the educational system in this country, we have no real vision of our capacity for greatness. Note: Most roles, not all roles played by Black male actors are of a nature that it typically involves making us laugh or are employed to entertain us; not to give us a positive view of the attributes of being a Black man. Because of this "seemingly inferior" self image, it serves as a fundamental need for the average working class Brother to scramble for some type of emotional cover.

This feeling of being inferior gives way for the growth of the "Macho" image projected by so many men today. Black men today are not taught the beauty of just being themselves. In social circles, he is not measured by the values of the times when men were just proud to be men. Times when a man was measured by the qualities of strength, character, and courage. Today he must drive the right car, not just **a** car, wear the **right** sneaker, and all that society has dictated to us. This is beginning at an earlier age than ever and if he does not acquire all these symbols of success, his image of himself is that of a total failure.

Another comparison Black men will usually make would be to celebrities or entertainers. Have you ever seen Black women at a Luther Vandross or Peabo Bryson concert? The reaction a Black man's woman may have is not always understood by the Black man. He longs to stimulate his woman to such levels of joy, he may even wonder, "if she had an opportunity to be intimate with these celebrities, even if only once, would she do so, or would she be faithful to him?" He falsely believes that he is inferior to these entertainers on a subconscious level and he will never be able to create this level of joy and this spills over into a feeling of just being inferior, period! Therefore, it will never happen, thus he makes a conscious choice to place his attention on other things. The reaction of his Black woman to the love songs performed by these entertainers is proof, in his eyes, that he is correct in his evaluation; this supports his feeling of inferiority. Typically after his best attempt at intimacy, the reaction he received was at best nil when compared to the enthusiasm his woman displayed at the concert or on other occasions. Thus he is steered further away from the concept of intimacy.

No one can exist in this world without interaction with people. With the advent of the women's movement, the Black man is faced with dealing with an educated and liberated woman that wants a sensitive man capable of being intimate. This is where the conflict arises. The Black man is now being asked to subject himself to the terror of humiliation by being intimate to acquire the love and affection of the Black woman he wants and needs desperately. For all the fine attributes this Black Angel may have, he cannot do it. He needs a little more information to help him break the pattern of his old behavior. Black men must come to understand and acknowledge first that they are human beings with feelings. Nothing can hurt as deep as losing a Black woman that you really love, so don't let it happen.

CHAPTER 3:

MOVING TOWARD UNDERSTANDING: KNOW WHAT HIS NATURAL INSTINCTS DICTATE TO HIM AND WHY?

"To know wisdom and instruction; perceive the words of understanding"-Proverbs 1:2

Did you know that a Black man more often than not, views his Black woman as an Angel? She is a blessing to him and he KNOWS IT! She is a gift from God and he holds her in the highest regard. He looks for her to be a driving force in his life each and everyday. He bestows honor upon her that is second to none. No other human being on earth experiences such joy and pleasure as a Black woman who **feels** loved by her Black man. In the beginning of a relationship, the Black woman knows this, she has a glow on her face that lets the world know that love is a wonderful experience. But, as time goes on she begins to change; you may see this same woman riding in a car with this same man and she looks different. She looks as though she has lost something very dear to her and you know what? She has. It is the hope and dream of an intimate relationship with this Black man she cares so deeply for. How did this happen? There is a very simple explanation for what has happened that has led to this unfortunate state of affairs. Simply stated, the Black woman does not know her man! He won't communicate with her and it is primarily because he cannot with the tools he has been given to work with.

There are a great many relationships that survive simply because there is security in surroundings that are familiar. There is no passion between the two, no enthusiasm, or feeling of connection; just a little bit of comfort knowing that a little bit of something is better than nothing at all. Black women today know this all too well due to the fact that there are so many more women than men. What she really desires is a relationship with passion, respect, and security. It is my feeling that she only need to understand what a Black man's natural instincts dictate to him.

A lot of dialogue is available about "women's intuition", but not about the natural instincts of men, the way we are made as human beings. It is extremely difficult for Black men today to survive in a relationship that is nurturing for the Black family unless his woman understands the state in which he lives, on a conscious, subconscious, and **instinctive** level of thought. If the pieces of the puzzle of life do not fit, then the world of the

Black man starts to break down. The study of this concept will be accompanied by several word descriptions for clarification.

For a long time now the Black man has been like a fish out of water, removed from his natural environment that provides him with all the essentials for his existence. When a fish is removed from his natural surroundings, the water, it begins to jump about in a frantic attempt to return itself to its home. As it begins to tire, its motion starts to diminish until eventually it lies there motionless. If left there, death is only moments away. Just like the fish, the Black man has been removed from his natural environment and left to die. What do I mean? Men especially Black men, have a natural instinct to fulfill their God-given responsibility to lead his woman and his family! He must be the head of his household, he must be in charge. **NOTE:** Many relationships and marriages work very well even when the woman is in charge and this is not to say that men must always be in charge, but just know that this is a natural instinct that most men do have; anything short of this and he is like a fish out of water, guaranteed a gradual, but certain loss of life! His inability to communicate with his woman is but a sign that he is slowly but steadily moving toward certain death. Communication is essential to growth for every human being and the only difference between that which is alive and that which is dead is GROWTH! That which lives is constantly changing, a little here, a little there, but it is growing. If the Black man isn't communicating, then he isn't growing, and if he isn't growing, then he must be dying, however slowly it may be.

This makes perfectly good sense to me and I am of total resolve to insure that we do not die.

WHAT DOES THE WORLD'S LEADING EXPERT SAY ABOUT OUR RELATIONSHIPS?

I have consulted with the world renowned expert on marriage and human relations to assist us in re-establishing our priorities and help us understand what our relationships should be like. I can offer no explanation as to why it works, how it works, I just know it works! Period. If you look at the state of things today verses fifty years ago, you don't have to be a rocket scientist to figure out that what we are doing now isn't working at all, not by any stretch of the imagination.

Many couples are locked in a power struggle over control in their relationship, why? To find an answer to this question, one must first be able and willing to fully accept the answer when it is found. Acceptance is probably the most difficult aspects of a relationship because we have been conditioned to respond negatively to things we do not agree with personally (see VIBRANT OPPOSITION Part 2). So often we seek the advice of the "experts" and do not agree with them or even understand why we are given certain advice or instructions, but we do not respond with such **vibrant** opposition as we do in our relationships. As a Black man, Proverbs 31:26, gives a very accurate picture of the expectation I personally have in a relationship with a Black woman; it states: "She openeth her mouth with wisdom; and in her tongue **is** the law of kindness." Any self-respecting Man whether he is Black or not, will lay his life on the line to protect his woman and defend her honor, I find it totally unacceptable to accept verbal abuse from someone I am willing to die for. This is instinctive, it is God given, it is how I am made, for that I will make no apologies.

In every relationship we all bring a certain level of gender expertise, yet we fail to take advantage of it. We have so many distractions today that in most cases we do not give our undivided attention to our mates, yet we listen to the so called experts, the doctors, lawyers, friends, etc.

"For a man indeed ought not to cover his head, forasmuch as he is the image and glory of God: But the woman is the **glory** of man." I Corinthians 11:7. This serves to confirm what the natural instinctive emotions are regarding how the Black man views his Angel. Can you relate this idea to a time when you felt this was true? When you first fell in love, when nothing else could give you such joy and happiness, that indescribable motion in your stomach? That feeling that let you know you are alive and wanted! These are the feelings of love and we ALL, long for them, especially Black men. To help us work through this it will be necessary to define glory, please find a dictionary and record the meaning.

GLORY:

How come we long for this thing called LOVE? Simply stated, it is one of the only things in life that can produce such intense states of pleasure! Nothing can compare to it, nothing can measure up to its moments of intense pleasure, I mean nothing. Have you ever heard a Black man say, "I don't need a woman."? If so it is a very rare occurrence because there is nothing that can take the place of a Black woman. If God made anything better than a Black woman, he kept it for himself.

It is my feeling that every Black woman has a right to know exactly where she stands in her man's life and it is for this reason that you owe it to yourself to ask your man this question, "is there anything that brings him more pleasure than you?" If your relationship is on unstable ground it may help you to get on with your life. Otherwise, it may generate some serious thought about his true feelings and attract him into intimacy. **ATTRACT HIM INTO INTIMACY**.

Let's look deeper into the concept of the natural instincts of Black men. How come there is this overwhelming desire to be in control of a relationship? Before addressing this issue let me make sure we have a clear understanding about the idea of "being in control or in charge" in a relationship. "I am not speaking from a position of being dominant or being allowed to mistreat a woman just because he is in charge. Another way to express this thought would be to say that he is concerned about the welfare of his Black Angel and his family, therefore, allowing his natural instincts, his instinctive ability to nurture and grow stronger. There are times when his instincts drive him to **seemingly** unacceptable limits of control and dominance. NOTE: *This is the rule rather than the exception and in no way attempts to suggest that a woman cannot "be in charge" because many relationships do exist successfully in an arrangement where the woman functions as the leader. The truth is that allowing a woman to "be in charge" goes against his natural instincts. Yes that's right; if you asked almost any Black man why he thinks he should be in charge, he won't be able to tell you specifically why it should be that way, however, he knows somehow that this is right and this is how he feels.*

Have you ever seen a bicycle built for two? You probably noticed that there are obviously two seats and only one person can ride on the forward most seat and steer the bicycle. Relationships must be structured in this same way; it must be built for two people to journey through life upon. In a relationship where two people are attempting to ride on the forward most seat and steer with the precision needed to arrive at the desired destination can prove to be a very difficult vehicle in which travel toward joy, happiness, and prosperity.

I have heard the typical argument between Black couples which usually has the man taking the position that, "it's my way or the highway" and the woman taking the position that, "I've got a mind of my own and the man cannot tell her what to do." It seems that the basis for this conflict lies in the arena that women accept without question the premise that "it is right for them to be able to do what they want because they do have a mind of their own." It is only fair to say that it really just comes down to what is appropriate and proper. Let me ask you, "would you go out and rob a bank just because you could?" If not, why not? It is probably due to the fact that it is against the law, right? Furthermore, would a mother let her child drink from a bottle of bleach just because the child has a mind of it's own? She is not a chemist or a biologist and she does not know the exact reactions that take place inside the body, but she does know that the manufacturer has warned her to keep this and other substances like it away from small children for their own protection. In other words, she heeds the warning of the experts and accepts their advice without question.

Well, I have consulted with the leading expert on human relations, God. God is an expert on life, love, joy, happiness, and prosperity to name a few. I submit to you that there are basic laws of nature established by God that govern human relationships. It is stated in 1 Corinthians 11:3, "But I would have you know, that the head of every man is Christ; and the head of every woman is the man; and the head of Christ is God." This is very simple and straight forward and it is my personal belief that there is a reason that it is stated so clearly. This particular arrangement within a relationship is so very instinctive to Black men and they know it in their hearts. They feel this way even though they can't explain it, it is our natural instinct as men. Again, understand that this reflects the rule rather than the exception, and some men will not find this to be true.

It is very important to understand that even if only on a subconscious level, that this is just as difficult for Black men to accept as it is for Black women to accept because the Black man has been conditioned to think so little of himself. Among many Black men there exists a deep level of self doubt and very low confidence; thus the Black man is afraid to be the one responsible for the welfare of one of God's Black Angels. Where has he learned or been taught anything that could give him a different point of view or position. You see, it is an awesome responsibility to be held accountable for the welfare of one of these Angels and her children, particularly in this society we live in today with all of the distractions and diversions. It can be a frightening proposition to many Black men. Understanding and accepting this is so vital to our survival; it is the means to our prosperity, and is the very spirit in which we must live each and every day. This is instinctive to the Black man whether or not he has seen this Scripture.

Let's review what we **KNOW:** first and foremost, (the focus for the Black man) we know that the woman is his glory; and secondly (the focus for the Black woman) we know that the man must answer to Christ for all that he does. I have stated it this way because the focus for the Black woman should not be that the man is the head of her, but the man does indeed have to answer to Christ for all that he does. Notice that there is a suggestion that the man a Black woman makes a choice to become involved with has a spiritual base because in Part Two of this text one of the ten reasons given for why relationships don't work today is the deterioration of the spiritual base in this society, thus when a man has a spiritual base he has rules that he plays the game of life by, he's in control and his life has balance. Therefore, a man that has a desire "to be in the driver's seat" that lives in acknowledgment of a spiritual creator will never knowingly or maliciously lead his Angel into danger or destruction. However, he is only human and will make mistakes, but he will surely learn more from his mistakes than his Angel will ever truly suffer. In the proper spirit of a loving and intimate relationship, two people should immediately try figure out how to recover from a mistake rather than beat each other down with insults and/or ridicule.

Now more than ever the Black man needs the trust of his Black Angel and the process must begin of attracting him into intimacy, for intimacy is an important ingredient in total freedom, mentally, emotionally, and spiritually. It is also important in strengthening the level of mutual respect and self respect. Let me make it perfectly clear that I love Black women far too much to advocate being a fool for the sake of "having a man", but it is very important for us to come to terms with what we must do, why we have to do it, and how we can do it. If you desire joy, happiness, and prosperity you now have the direction in which to travel to achieve this state of existence.

To all my Brothers, you must accept full responsibility for the welfare of our Black women and their children for we **will** answer to Christ when all is said and done. Black women are fortunate in that they only have to answer to us, as God has directed, and since she **is** our glory, her life should be comfortable and filled with joy and happiness, RIGHT? If you truly desire to be more intimate with your woman and don't know where to begin, start by telling her how much she really means to you and how sorry you are for all the things you've put her through. Our Sisters have put up with far too much from us for far too long now, if we are truly the men we think we are then let's start by having our actions mirror or reflect our real feeling.

In closing this chapter I want to say, both Black men and Black women are creations of God. That makes us both equal human beings. Although we are on the same team and on the same playing field, we have two distinct and different roles or positions to play, neither one being superior to or more important than the other, they are just different. There would be no team or game without both people involved! This is not what I say personally, it is what God says and I think we owe it to ourselves to let God's way work for us. As living, thinking, rational, and compassionate beings created by God, we know in our hearts it could not possibly be worse than what we have going on now, can it? In addition, 1 Corinthians 11:14 does suggest that the Black man does indeed have natural instincts, it reads as follows: "Doth not nature itself teach you, that if a man have long hair, it is a shame unto him?" (Food for thought, does not every picture you've ever seen that was supposed to be "Jesus" show a man with long hair? I just found that strange!) But this does bring to light another concern and that is, we need to get all the Brothers out of the beauty shops and back into the barber shops for we have far too much to do to spend two or three hours "getting our hair done" like a woman does. Get out of the mirror, stop trying to compete with the women trying to look pretty, for we can never look as good as our Sisters and we should not want to. Make yourself presentable, take good care of yourself and let's tend to our business at hand, being men. Understanding our natural instincts can be a starting point which will lead toward intimacy and discovering the true self; we must take full advantage of these instincts for they are what lead us and guide us, they can and will work for us if we let them. How else would we know what profession or career to choose? Isn't that an instinct at work?

CHAPTER 4:

THE BLACK MAN: HIS EGO AND EMOTIONS

I read an article in a newspaper about the inability of men to be intimate, which included excerpts from an interview with a male psychologist who stated, that men could not connect words with their feelings. The author stated, that men could not get in touch with their feelings or express emotions. I must say, if you have ever done something to "tick or piss" a Black man off, he will surely get in touch with his feelings very quickly and let you know in a very clear way that he does feel. He will connect plenty of words with his emotions, many of which cannot be used in the context of this material, but I am sure you get the picture, therefore, I dismissed this notion and do not buy into that school of thought.

This notion that men are not in touch with their feelings or express emotions, holds true only with respect to certain emotions and when it involves direct communication with a woman. If you have ever been to a baseball, football, basketball, or hockey game you have witnessed men being very emotional.

Men, particularly, Black men, by nature are very emotional creatures. They write beautiful love ballads, they sing them, they feel them deep down inside. When a Black man is with his Black woman he will play these love songs for her as a way to help him express his own feelings. To my Sisters, the next time you hear or he plays a love song that you know he likes, ask him if he feels that way about you. Does he like this song because it strengthens his feelings about you? This may open up lines of communication that you didn't even know existed, let alone connected! Black entertainers are capable of arousing Black women to very intense states of joy and happiness through the delivery of a love ballad. The Black man indeed has the desire to arouse his woman to such levels, but it is very difficult to overcome the fear of failing to do so.

He may be listening to Luther Vandross or Peabo Bryson while he is with his woman and feels the emotions he wants to express, but I am sure we can all agree these are tough acts to follow; so now his subconscious takes over and says to him, "are you nuts, we don't stand a chance of coming close to that!" Typically most men will retreat into themselves not taking a chance on failure or loss of respect. I can only attempt to convey what it would mean for the Black man to be rejected in his attempt at moving toward intimacy with his Black Angel. To be perceived as corny or unromantic, to be laughed at, called silly, no matter how innocent, would be completely devastating for him. Most Black men won't take that chance because the fear is absolutely overwhelming!!! His ego is far too fragile to subject it to this possible humiliation. However, if over time he receives enough assurance and support and is in his natural environment he can and probably will overcome this fear of being humiliated, but only if there is enough trust! There can be no excuses for not being intimate with the Black woman. She has a fundamental need for intimacy that is vital to her peace of mind and security, as does the Black man, but his need is just not as intense. We only have to learn what buttons to push to open up the lines of communication and connect them.

Most Black men are very fragile deep down inside. Unfortunately, most of their emotional pursuits are misdirected, in that they are away from the very person that rightfully deserves to receive them -- his Black Angel! Question, "how come many men will spend countless hours washing their car or playing sports, but won't invest one hour to come home draw the bath water for their Angel and give her a bath?" Where did we learn how to place value on the things in our lives? What dictates the way we prioritize our lives? Instead of pouring out his emotions at sporting events and the like, he **MUST** spend a **GREAT** deal more time involving himself in dialogue with his Angel. To the Black men, you must know that this is where the quality of life begins to escalate, everything about you will be elevated, your professional, social, and personal life will be enriched through this experience. However, it is a conscious choice (see definition below) you must make and make fast for if you choose to remain an intimate introvert, you will die, both emotionally and spiritually. Become balanced, take in love and give love!

CHOICE: *An option selected from several alternatives for pursuit as a course of self-determination, whereby most of your attention and/or energy is directed in such a way that results are measurable on a daily basis. Note: If an individual cannot monitor his actions and make a definitive decision as to its effectiveness, then chances are they are not committed or they may need to change their option, i.e. If in a relationship, your desired result is to have peace and harmony, and this is not what you are getting, then you may have look at your root causes that create this environment.*

To the Black Angels I will ask this question, have you ever said to a Black man, "I don't need you, I can do bad by myself"? I have never been told this, but, I have a great imagination and I cannot think of too many things that could bring such gut-wrenching pain than to hear someone that is supposed to be my **glory,** my Angel say this to me. I would be completely devastated, it would numb me all the way down to the soles of my feet. It would leave me feeling very empty inside, with a feeling so close to worthlessness. Imagine being called into your supervisor's office where you work. Your supervisor says, "I must inform you that we don't need you." That's it, no letter, no request for your resignation, just that statement.

Think for a moment, what do you think or imagine you would feel inside? Would you leave with a feeling of confidence, high self-esteem, security, and self-worth? Keep in mind that these statements are usually made during a time when there's already a great deal of pain in the moment, therefore saying this only tends to magnify its intensity and impact. Record your thoughts and feelings. Do you find this scenario conducive to attracting a man into intimacy?

Let's look at where relationships typically end up emotionally. They seem to arrive at a state where both people are hanging on to each other until they can do better. The Black man is usually in a pretty intense state of isolation which undoubtedly is created by circumstances outside of the relationship. Unfortunately, he will bring some of these negative feelings and beliefs into his relationship with his Black woman. These negative feelings are personalized and become a part of his belief system. If there are any problems or situations that threaten his ego or "manhood" this magnifies his feelings of isolation, fear, and insecurity in a relationship he is already uncomfortable with.

The emotional isolation for the Black man can be overwhelming, for there are no role models, or should I say very few for Black men to connect with emotionally; this is especially true for younger Black males. It seems that many Black men choose to become involved with white women once they have reached a certain level of success, leaving the Black man that prefers Black women somewhat confused. I often wondered during the hearings of Judge Clarence Thomas if in fact a large part of his trouble did stem from the fact that he was married to a white woman. I do not have a problem with what another man does with his relationships, but what does concern me is the subtle message that says, you have not really made it unless you have a white woman.   The Black woman isn't worthy. What did all these Brothers do before they could be intimate with white women? I accept the premise that love has no color barriers, but just the same there are subconscious messages we receive, whether we acknowledge them or not, they are there. Have you ever noticed that when a Black man and white woman are together in public, that one or both will usually have a smile on their face? What would you think this suggests subconsciously? Is it easier for a Black man to be intimate with a white woman? Absolutely! Why do I say this? Primarily I would suggest to you that it is easier for the average Black man that cannot do the latest dances to attempt to dance in a room full of white people than in a room full of Black people. Why? It is easier to be uninhibited, to let go in an environment that is unfamiliar. I suspect that the white woman expects the Black man to be different, and that the Black man wants to be different, thus this an attractive proposition for him.

In general, people live up to what is expected of them. That's probably one very good reason why you rarely if ever see a Black woman with a poor white man-she expects him to have money and he usually does! For the record "a Black woman is certainly good enough to be called my Mother, and a Black woman is more than worthy of being my wife!" Where would we be as a people without the love and devotion of Black women? This why Black men must start being intimate and let the Black Angels know exactly how we feel so they may be happy.

Black men have been given an image that says they cannot or do not express their emotions. Unfortunately, it is my perception that Black men commit more crimes of passion than do Black women; I may have to be corrected on this for I do not have any statistics to support this position, but just the same it is my perception. I said that, to say this, the Black man is capable of expressing his emotions, he has just been conditioned to express the wrongs ones. His avenues of expression are simply misdirected as a result of his experiences and environment. Today, it seems the younger they are the more misdirected they turn out to be.

The influence of our past experiences and moments sometimes govern our present moment and serve to destroy any chance that we may have for joy and happiness now. Each and every day we all have plans, desires, and expectations of what we want in our lives, things that we want to do, places we want to go, things we would like to acquire. However, as we all know, things do not always go our way. Things get "all screwed up."

At these particular moments, of trials and tribulations, we sometimes let it affect our spirit, our disposition, our attitude, and our relationships, whether it be in business or our personal life. We may be down right angry as a result of something or someone that is totally unrelated to the person or situation we are dealing with at the moment, it did not just happen, it is not happening now, but it did occur in time, a moment before now and we drag it or bring it forward into the present moment. It is unfair to yourself, to others, and is very unhealthy and destructive to live this way. Think of it this way, if you prepared oatmeal in a pot for breakfast, could you use the same pot to prepare chicken noodle soup for lunch? My point being, of course you could, but chances are you **would AFTER** you cleaned the pot, removed the oatmeal!   In other words, before you begin to communicate with anyone, but particularly your Black man or Black woman, **WASH OUT YOUR POT**, remove any negatives thoughts or feelings that might ruin your recipe for that special moment with someone you care deeply for.   This will keep you from inflicting emotional discomfort on some poor soul who has done absolutely nothing to deserve it, except happen to be near you. It will literally make a difference in every aspect of your life, but does not just happen, it takes practice.

This leads me to the focal point which has driven me to address this concept of intimacy and Black men, the Black woman-the one with the power to change the course of history from this day forward. To all of the beautiful Black Angels I will say this,

"Where you go the men will follow!" Night club owners know this all too well; I'm sure you are familiar with a concept called "Ladies Night", right? This is not done strictly out of appreciation or admiration, it is done because it is more profitable to the business owner. Men of business know that if you bring in the ladies, the men will follow and that translates into dollars because they now have the heavy drinkers in the house, the men.

In every city I have traveled to, I have noticed the care and pride Black women take in their appearance. They know the way they look gives them power! Something they probably don't know is that they could wage a war on crime and drugs in America that would render the effort put forth by law enforcement and the government absolutely meaningless and entirely useless. What may be even harder to believe is that it would not cost one thin dime! Sounds impossible doesn't it? But remember, where you go, the men will follow! If all of the Black Angel's simply demanded that any Black man they decide to become involved with be lawful and sober, you would see another level of life as we now know it. As effective as I know this would be, it still isn't as easy as it sounds because it would involve a tremendous shift in the value system we have come to accept from this European society we have been raised in. But we still must know how we can improve the quality of life in our own communities for the welfare of our families. We must keep this in our thoughts and strive to connect ourselves with

God; to receive his wisdom and instruction, then accept his gift of life! Black men and women are equal, we are both creations of God, but we are different and have different roles to play in life. We must accept these roles unconditionally.

A Black man will do more for his Angel than he will for himself, I suspect that it has to do with the fact that just by our very nature we are so far removed from our true and total being. That is why more often than not, it is a Black Angel that can put a Black man on the right track; this must not be taken out of the true context in which all things come through God, but remember the Black woman is a blessing to the Black man just by his very nature. Most of the things the Black man will do he will do ultimately to score points with the Black woman, to impress her, to win her affection. This is why the value system and the moral code of the Black woman must be beyond the worldly things of this society.

Vast numbers of Black men, both young and old, are moving about society everyday ingesting drugs into their bodies to try and eliminate the pain of life, which in most cases is of an emotional nature. That is why crack cocaine is so very dangerous to our communities and our survival because of its ability to change a persons mental state from one of overwhelming pain to one of euphoria, **FAST!** Faster than anything that will probably ever be known to man. This is a tragedy because it can be eliminated or removed from the lives of so many of these Brothers without drug treatment plans that just leave the individual looking for a replacement, some other form of addiction. Drugs and other chemicals are a wicked way of life, but remember, Happy people are **never** wicked! Happiness as a way of life is the order of the day, starting right now. Developing patience is an absolute must for every Black man and woman in order for us to receive what we desire and deserve out of life. The same patience we show outside of our relationships, we must bring into our relationships.

We must understand that many of our young Brothers and old alike, are not dealing drugs in our neighborhoods for the money they receive. Sounds crazy doesn't it? Consider this, these Brothers are not lazy, it is not that they do not want to work. If you look at the conditions they work under and the hours they put in, you will see it has nothing to do with being lazy. In all cases it would be far easier and more rewarding to get a job or start a legitimate business. Then why do they do it? The answer is at least a two part proposition. First, we have been conditioned to fulfill **ALL** of our wants **NOW**. The things that we need can wait, **AI want what I want and I want it now!** Secondly, and probably more of a driving factor is that Black men are on these streets selling drugs because the money gets the material things that many Black women **desire**; money buys the things they need to impress women with. In-other-words, it buys the things that are **impressed** upon the Black women by society. That is why you will rarely see a drug dealer that doesn't have his share of Black and/or white women to choose from. He can attract them into a relationship. This is why bringing a message to Black women is so important because there is security in numbers. You have the power to point the Black man in the right direction. The power is right between your ears and in your heart, using your mind and your heart you can decide what your priorities should be, what decisions you can make, and what should you believe?

This society we live in today says that men and women are "equal." Let's look at the psychological impact of just how crazy this notion really is. God has given women the ability to carry a child in her womb, not men. Men cannot bare children and it would be insane for them to run around demanding their right to do so, just because they too are human beings and should be considered equal. We must all be who and what we were born to be, period! Just by nature, things affect men and women in very different ways, we must understand this. Let us begin to dismiss the notion in our relationships as to which individual is correct and entertain the notion of what would be or what is correct for a given situation to achieve happiness. After all isn't that what we all really want, to just be happy? We are equal, not identical, we are different!

The Black man does not need pity because of his condition or circumstances, nor does he need sympathy; what he needs is a Black Angel that will extend to him the respect that he deserves and she must receive respect in return. This will put some fire under his behind and wake him up. His Black Angel must be with him in spirit and she must know how to let things happen by being in step with the natural order of life itself. This can and will happen only after the Black man makes being intimate with his Black Angel a top priority, something that must be done, just as we must have food to eat, clothes to wear, and air to breathe. The Black man must develop a strong level of self-acceptance and with the love and respect of his Black Angel he will be able to numb the pain and regain his ability to function as a strong and positive force in society.

CHAPTER 5:

WHAT DO BLACK MEN WANT FROM BLACK WOMEN?

I've touched bases on how the Black man feels about his Black Angel, now I want to address the question of what he wants and expects from the Black woman. Personally, I think foremost Black men want to be happy and to have good clean fun. Fun in the traditional sense. For this one I will supply the definition fun: 1) a pleasant diversion or amusement; highly enjoyable recreation; sport, 2) lighthearted playfulness; gaiety. With the right mental attitude, for a Black man, just coming home from work to be with his woman can definitely qualify as fun, a pleasant diversion, highly enjoyable. I might add, it is a must that this become the reality for all Black men and women because for many Black men upon entering his kingdom, his castle, his home, if he does not find this "fun" here, he will be leaving not long after his arrival to find it.

Having fun does not necessarily mean spending big bucks. I have had the most fun at times when I've spent the least amount of money.   The most fun I've ever had was a time when I only had twenty-five cents in my pocket and believe it or not I did not even spend that! So I know it can be done, that it is possible.

Life has become so serious, such an event of competition, that we have lost our ability to have fun, to be vulnerable to the opportunity, to allow it to happen. Do we always have fun when we are supposed to? What things do we do strictly for fun? When was the last time we were able to laugh at ourselves because we did something that we thought was funny? My point is of course, that it is impossible to experience anything but **happiness** when we are having fun. No matter what you do make the relationship fun to be in each and every day. Learn to smile on a regular basis, it work wonders.

I think it is extremely important to understand that femininity is a breeding ground for intimacy when coupled with positive dialogue from the Black woman. Black women are very sexy and most any man of any race, creed, or color will tell you this, therefore naturally Black men are very responsive to the sight of a beautiful Black Angel.   This aspect of their being is closely associated to femininity, to being an Angel. The Black man looks for everything that his Angel does to be consistent with his image of her. He expects the sound of her voice to be sweet and latent with the sounds that let him know she is indeed an Angel. However, we know this is not always the case.

I feel it is almost impossible to create an environment that is intimate with a Black man when he is constantly put down and criticized for being himself, Black men expect to be accepted as they are, as they were in the beginning of the relationship. It is very disturbing to Black men to hear his Angel use language that is not consistent with the Angelic image he has of her. We're not talking an occasional slip of the tongue as an added touch in general conversation, or to add humor. Instead, what we're talking about is profanity as a primary language. Excessive profanity does not become a beautiful Black Angel. It shatters the Angelic image a Black man has of the Black woman in his mind. Profanity when used in conjunction with a nasty and demeaning tone can give rise to a very hostile environment in which nobody progresses. (See Part 2, The Power Of Words)

Most Black men grew up in homes that were void of women using any kind of abusive language directed at the Black man from the Black woman. Women of the era, out of sheer respect for the man, just simply did not behave this way. Not that is should make a difference, but there seems to have been a lot less domestic violence when women shared this point of view. Since have I reached the subject of violence, let me quickly address it. My personal advice to any Black man finding himself being physically abusive to his Black woman is this, understand that it is against your very nature to treat the glory of your life in this manner. There is something very wrong with your analysis of the situation as to the most effective way to resolve conflict or differences, you are sick and you need help. Seek help, find help, and by all means use it. My advice to Black women finding themselves in this situation of being abused is this, demand that this man get the help he needs immediately. Take a very good look at the elements that were responsible for creating this situation and then eliminate them from your relationship because if there are elements that create a hostile environment, then there are elements that create a loving peaceful one as well. If this Black man really loves you and respects you then seeking help to stop the abuse will not be a problem, likewise, what ever it is that you can do to bring peace and love will not be a problem either. You can trust me on this, if he is violent toward you, <u>there **is** a problem</u> and if he objects to getting help, get out immediately. However, if you decide to stay in the relationship and allow him to seek help you must be able to forgive and forget.

An important ingredient in the recipe for happiness is the ability to forgive and **forget.** One without the other is just another way of saying, "I'll put this matter in layaway!" When you put something in layaway you are in debt, you typically will receive some sort of statement reminding you that you have an item that you will own in the future and must pay for in full. Look up the definition of forgive, you see, if you say that you will forgive, but not forget, what you are saying is contradictory. If you say that you forgive someone, then its over, the past is just that, the past. The subject will be closed and sealed never to be brought up again. Then you will be free to enjoy today.

Always keep in your thoughts, wash out that pot, so the next meal (moment) will be enjoyable.

READ THROUGH THIS CAREFULLY, PLEASE!

<u>ALL WORK IS HONORABLE!</u>

All work is honorable, as it relates to the Black man means that it is totally irrelevant and extremely presumptuous to think of a Black man as a "good catch" or "legitimate prospect" just because he wears particular clothes or has a fancy title and can babble on using a battery of fifty cent words that collectively mean absolutely nothing. I've witnessed on more occasions than I care to remember, a hard working, decent, and caring Black man have his pride smashed and his ego crushed simply because he enjoys doing a certain kind of work, or due to circumstances ends up doing a particular kind of work.   A Black man should be judged not on what he does for a living, but how he does what he does for a living, this tells his true spirit. As African people, we need to study our own history to understand who we really are and where we come from to help us return our focus to that which is our own. To make this short and sweet, let me put it this way: "a kind, gentle, and caring man that delivers pizza for a living will bring more joy and happiness into your life than some buzzard in fancy clothes that you **imagine** to be Mr. Right.   Food for thought: a man with big bucks can just about get any woman he wants and he really does not have to put forth much effort, he lets his material assets do most of his talking. In many cases, it gets the job done.

I have always maintained close relationships with women over the years and I have always been there to help them pick their hearts up after some man has dropped it and smashed it cold! If a Black man honors you, and treats you like the Angel that you are, stop and think twice before you concern yourself with what he does for a living. I submit to you if he treats you like dirt and breaks your pretty little heart, would you say, "you no good, low-down, dirty, Doctor?" I think not, you would call him a **"DOG!"** Why? Because at this point what he does for a living, where he lives, how much money he spends on you, or even the kind of car he drives, is totally irrelevant, just as it should have been from the beginning. Black men expect, need, and want to feel important, loved, and worthy for who they are and what they are, human beings with feelings!

PART 2

INGREDIENTS
FOR A SUCCESSFUL
RELATIONSHIP

THE WORKSHOP

SECTION 1: THE FOUNDATION

In 1979 God spoke to my heart and said, "you are with me now, just sit back, relax, and enjoy the journey." He took me where I **needed** to go, not where I thought I should go. For that I give praise.

Donald E. Law

A RECIPE FOR LIVING

(A simple philosophy of life)

Everything that happens to me is in God's plan. I am where I am today because this is where God wants me to be, if this were not true I would be somewhere else, doing something else. My purpose is to find out why I am here now.

All thoughts come from somewhere, if I receive a good thought today, I will pursue it with command authority, WHY NOT? I have pursued enough bad one's to last me the rest of my life.

I have two choices every day when I wake up, I can be happy or I can be sad, it's a matter of choice. I simply choose to be happy, WHY NOT?

There are two kinds of people I allow in my life, people with a positive attitude and millionaires. (SMILE)

I do not argue, it's a waste of time. 999 times out of 1000 I will not change a persons point of view, I will accept the difference and move to something more constructive and rewarding.

I do not live in the past, it's a waste of time. The past is over and nothing I think about with respect to it will ever change it. I will learn from the past and leave it there. I cannot successfully look in two directions at the same time, if I am looking backwards I cannot be looking ahead.

I like to refer to Black women as God's Black Angels and I make no apologies for that because they are God's creations. Black women are extremely precious and have incredible power. Black women must feel their worth, period. Let me qualify what I've just said by this, Black women have given birth to **EVERY** great Black man that has ever lived, that's special.

Most women I've talked with have expressed to me that they strongly feel that a man will do anything to gain access to sleeping with them, I submit to you today that if this is true, he will even do the right thing **if** placed in his natural environment. Brothers we must learn to treat one woman right first, with honor, respect, dignity, and not just as a sperm depository! There is much more to our Angel's than that.

Do you know who I am? I am the guy you knew in high school or even junior high. Remember me? The guy who didn't wear the fancy clothes or have all the cool and slick rap lines that Brothers hit on girls with. Come on now think for a minute, I'm sure you will remember me? Well maybe not because you didn't give me the time of day because I am that Nerd! (Review Chapter 5) You can find a GOOD BLACK MAN, if you just get clear a few fundamental dynamics about the nature of our existence and accept a few fundamental truths about life. What experiences have we had that make up our value system. Why do we believe what we believe? i.e., Some women believe all men are dogs, is it because we look like and sound like dogs? or is it because we behave like dogs, engaging in sex randomly, without thought or feeling? I would suspect that it is the latter.

This is where it is absolutely essential for intimate communication to exist, in developing the understanding of the other person and putting the pieces of the puzzle together which answers the question, why do we do what we do? The predominate force or factor in us is our desire to protect ourselves from emotional suffering or either to enjoy ourselves and have fun in life. Understanding this allows us to exist in a state of awareness even if we do not completely understand why a situation or condition is present in our relationship.

Regarding finding the information we use to better our relationships, if I had to make an analogy, it would be of an automobile that has run out of gas, and the owner has a broken gas gauge, but doesn't know at the moment. You know the car (or the relationship) isn't working, but you don't know that it's out of gas. Once you figure out it's the gauge that is faulty and it just needs gas, it really doesn't matter whether you fill the tank with Exxon, Amoco, or Shell. But you must put fuel into the tank to make it run. Love and respect are the fuels that make the relationship run. Communication, excellent spirit, and a sound philosophy are the additives that will allow a relationship to run at peak performance. Simply making an automobile's gas tank bigger won't make it go any faster.

What most brothers have been taught about how to treat a woman

1) You don't hit girls.

2) The more women you have the more of a man you are.

SECTION 2 : COMMUNICATION

THE POWER OF WORDS

"IN THE BEGINNING GOD CREATED THE HEAVEN AND THE EARTH"

Genesis 1:1

The active word in the above statement is "created" meaning that the only way to have a loving environment is to create it using the power of words. The power of words is truly awesome! Words can:

EXPRESS EMOTIONS
BE DESTRUCTIVE
BE CONSTRUCTIVE
CREATE ECONOMIC OPPORTUNITY

A quote from *THINK AND GROW RICH A BLACK CHOICE* by Dennis Kimbro and Napoleon Hill, chap. 8, pg 196 par. 1 says, "Don't criticize, condemn, or complain. Any fool can criticize, condemn, or complain-and most fools do. But it takes character and self-control to be understanding and forgiving. Instead of condemning others, try to understand them. Figure out why they do what they do. That's more profitable and intriguing than criticism; it breeds sympathy, tolerance, and kindness."

VIBRANT OPPOSITION
THE INTIMACY ELIMINATOR

The sound of constant opposition over a period time begins to generate useless negative emotions and isolation, nobody really loves to be wrong. Therefore, each time we see the person that is directing some type of negative verbal assault, we go into a state that is so mentally negative and our spirit is pulled down. Our attitude is negative. After all, do we wake up each day with enthusiasm to find out how many times we can be wrong? I liken the sound of constant opposition to finger nails being scraped across a chalkboard or someone popping gum. It becomes very irritating and it creates a hostile and unnatural environment. Black men today are like a fish out of water, removed from their natural environment, if we remain in this state death is the only option.

Proverbs 31:26 states, "She openeth her mouth with wisdom; and in her tongue **is** the law of kindness." Again, as we look at the natural instincts of a Black man, it may start to become evident that it indeed goes against the instinctive perception or that gut feeling when our Angel displays behavior contrary to that of wisdom and kindness in her dialogue. It cannot be stressed enough about the power of words, we must start now to increase our awareness daily with respect to how we select and use the power of words to create a more loving and compassionate atmosphere in which we live. One's state of awareness, is just like a muscle, each time we exercise it a little each day, it becomes stronger and stronger. Once we have sufficiently strengthened our ability to be alert, aware, or concentrate, we can begin to deny the negative forces that surround us by choosing to concentrate on what we choose to.

It is human nature to avoid any situation that will bring about an emotional state that is very uncomfortable, such as a Black man being constantly put down or criticized. Most Black men will be driven to seek an environment that will allow him to be more at ease and feel special, an environment with fewer negative memories to reflect upon. In live workshops, women often ask, "why do men cheat on them." I usually cite three major reasons why men are so unfaithful. First and foremost, because women allow it. I submit to you that if I am in a relationship with a woman and she finds it necessary to be with another man, it will only happen one time and one time only. People put up with what they want to put up with. Secondly, in many cases men are literally driven away because the environment they are in provides no understanding, comfort, or peace of mind. And finally, Black women must understand just how desirable they are to begin with, you are so very beautiful, warm, and dedicated that our very nature makes it difficult for us to not want to be with you. That is why it is so very important that Black women learn to create a warm environment for their Black man to be in. If not, this makes having more than one woman an attractive proposition. Furthermore, many times a woman may have done anything and everything to make a beautiful home for her Black man only to be left in total disbelief to find out that he has been seeing someone else. She may even refer to him as a "dog." He cannot begin to explain his behavior because he has absolutely no idea what has driven him to act this way, but he does know that he is wrong. He also knows, deep down inside that he will pay a heavy price for his actions. How many times have we as Black men really done wrong and sincerely apologized and asked to be forgiven? If we as Brothers can find the time, energy, and desire to be better mates <u>after</u> we have screwed up, then we can certainly find these same elements or ingredients before we mess up. Remember, if we can find the love and understanding after we mess up, we can find that same love and understanding and get it right the first time so we can allow our Sister's to show their true beauty. We cannot afford to be trapped by the many distractions today, let us learn to focus more directly on one another exclusively from the beginning when we are with them. It is my fundamental belief that anything can be created with the positive use of the power of words or the omission/avoidance of the negative use the power of words possesses. We must accept the power that words possess and respect them. Words, once released in the form of a negative thought or feeling, in many cases cannot be retrieved.

WHAT DO OUR NATURAL INSTINCTS DICTATE TO US AS ADULT MALES? We as Black men expect the voices of our Angel's to be latent with the sweet sounds consistent with the Angelic image that naturally comes with being a man. As stated in the Scriptures "For a man indeed ought not to cover his head, forasmuch as he is the image of God: but the woman is the glory of the man", I Corinthians 11:7. I have discussed this concept with an awful lot of Brothers and I have yet to find one that will disagree with this. Every Brother feels that this is our very nature, that is how we are made. We instinctive feel this way, yet I'm sure we can all agree that if you have not personally experienced a relationship contrary to this, you at least know a Sister that has been mistreated by a Brother. How can this be true then? Just being able to effectively express our thoughts and feelings in a warm environment is an important step in developing the kind of relationship we all desire. Many things affect our ability to effectively communicate in a relationship, such as arguments. Just know that arguments are: disagreements with very intense emotions, if you remove the intensity of the emotions you just have a simple disagreement, which most everyone can live with. Cool heads must prevail, if not two heads, at least one person in the relationship must be the designated peace keeper. This person is primarily responsible for knowing when to shut up and let things cool down. I suggest that this be the responsibility of the man, Proverbs 17:28 "Even a fool, when holdeth his peace, is counted wise: **and** he that shutteth his lips is **esteemed** a man of understanding." **REMEMBER WASH OUT YOUR POT!**

I once heard a story about a little boy and a little girl, the boy was about 4 and the little girl was about 5 and they were taking a bath together. The little girl looked at the little boy and said, "what's that?" The little boy responded, "that's my boat silly!" The little girl, pointing to the old family jewels of the little boy, said "no, that!" The little boy said, "I don't know." The little girl said, "can I touch it." Confused, the boy looked down at himself, then looked at the little girl and said, "heck no, you broke yours off already!" I tell this story because men and women are fundamentally different. Men and women communicate with a different language and understand things from a different perspective, women feel expressions of love, i.e. cards and gifts vs. the manly way to show love. On a personal level: due to my aptitude for mechanics I love things with motors and switches and stuff. Consequently when I would go to by gifts, I'd naturally be impressed with things that had, guess what? Things that light up, make noise with motors and switches and stuff. Food processors, blenders, electric shavers, etc. I can remember always thinking, wow, she's got to love this. I would be excited at the prospect of how much I knew she would like this gift. WRONG! Women respond to things they can feel, men respond to things that are more or less tangible, i.e. tone of a woman's voice, trust or things that indicate the lack of such as looking through his wallet. In relationships we must be bilingual, we must be able to speak and understand in both languages, **this is very important.**

When communication becomes strained make sure definitions are clear. Sometimes, and I think this is extremely important, we must make a few assumptions in our relationships. When we are communicating with our partners, we must understand that they primarily do not want to put us in pain. I cannot begin to tell you how many times I've experienced in a relationship, having said something and had the meaning of my statement completely misunderstood. This is where many of our problems arise because we do not exercise the patience and strive for the same understanding in our relationships that we do outside of them. When we are in school or at work, we take the time to understand problems, but we become impatient and even down right rude with our mates. To me, it's a matter what we are willing to do to have a lasting and nurturing relationship. If we desire it, make the decision that you will have it, be very attentive to what **you** are doing, and do not settle for anything short of being happy.

THE RELATIONSHIP AS A COIN!

On one side of the coin is Love and on the other side is Respect. We will describe love as the feelings you have for a person and define respect as the way you treat a person as a result of the feelings you have for them. Therefore, if you profess to love a person make sure that you make it known through your actions. Make sure you do not confuse admiration for respect.

Any discussion of this nature would be incomplete without the inclusion of teamwork in a relationship. Personally, and this is good ole Donald talking, I have never believed that there is such a thing as a 50-50 relationship. The problem with this concept is that it is at least implied that there exists finite or terminal point where one can stop giving to a relationship. To me this is a completely ridiculous notion. Both people in the relationship must carry their share of the load given his or her situation at the moment. There are no part-time positions available in the business of love. Both people must be willing to give 100% of themselves 100% of the time. Success in a relationship hinges upon desire, patience, respect, love, commitment, kindness, and consideration. In order for two people to exist in a relationship, they must understand the other person's dynamic personality. In other words, know what makes them tick, know why they do what they do. We must work together, live together, and be happy together.

SECTION 3: RESPECT IN A RELATIONSHIP

RESPECT EARNED (This aspect shuts out more good Brother's because they never are given a chance because someone before them screwed up **BIG TIME!**) Any discussion

65

on understanding the Black man would be bogus without the inclusion of the concept or issue of respect earned vs. respect extended. I liken the extension of respect in a relationship to that of being pregnant, you either are or you are not. Respect is either present or it is not, there is nor can there be any area in between. Many people have been conditioned to have minimal respect for the Black man and there is a serious problem of the perception society projects of the Black man that we must be aware of.

I wish to focus in on the relationship as it relates to respect. I firmly believe that no man can dig himself out of a hole by digging it deeper. Often I've heard people say that a person has to earn their respect. In most cases it is my feeling that women have always suffered far more emotional discomfort in relationships than do men, therefore, more often than not they arrive at a point where they are not as likely to trust a man from the outset of the relationship. They carefully observe the man and his behavior looking for any information that will support her position that he should not be trusted. If we do not extend mutual respect in the beginning of a relationship, then we will inhibit the level of intimacy that is potentially available. If an individual goes into a relationship and has to earn respect, they start out in a hole. Now instead of being handed a ladder which represents forgiveness for the mistakes that all people make, they are given a shovel which represents the mistakes, thus each time a mistake is made the hole is dug a little deeper. Black men are very aware of this situation if only on a

66

subconscious level. Being in this situation is a no win proposition the Black man will conclude, if I am human and I make a mistake, I lose. IN ADDITION, THERE IS THE PRESUPPOSITION THAT HE IS NOT WORTHY OF RESPECT. HOW CAN ANYONE COME FROM SO FAR BEHIND AND EXPECT TO BE SUCCESSFUL?

SECTION 4:

WHERE THE RUBBER MEETS THE ROAD!
10 REASONS WHY RELATIONSHIPS DON'T WORK?

#1

There is a deterioration of the spiritual base in this society that has given rise to the omission of this aspect of our relationships. There is a tremendous gap in the fundamental beliefs of the two people involved. I might suggest that next time a man asks you out on a date, make it Sunday morning and take him to church!

#2

We abandon our principles to get the one we want. We allow our rules to be broken or compromised. I.e., If your rules and/or principles say, drugs and alcohol are inappropriate, then it should also be inappropriate to become intimate with someone who does. I've said for years, "I'm not opposed to drugs or alcohol, but I am opposed to what people do under their influence."

#3

We spend far too much time in La La Land and don't find out who we are really dealing with. In other words the person we start out with is not the same person we end up with! Communication at this stage is very critical, usually vital information about the person is revealed, yet is many times ignored. Also know that many people are not really focused on the fact they just really don't want to be alone, so they tend to stay in very unhealthy relationships.

#4

We simply choose the wrong person and attract the kind of people that are not good for us. I. e., For me when I examined the relationships that ended up as a total disaster I found that the one thing that they all had in common was that I was involved with aggressive women, women that came after me in a very strong way and they were also verbally very aggressive. This is what I attracted, but this is not the kind of woman that I am compatible with.

#5

Sex is given too high of a priority in the relationship.

#6

THIS IS CRITICAL

Black women are the only source of happiness and joy that Black men can turn to. When we are with our women we as Black men have a fundamental understanding that this is the only place we can feel special. If we do not experience this special feeling inside our relationship, we will typically go outside of the relationship to find this place where we will feel special. What I want to share with the Brothers in particular at this moment is that you can show a woman in as many ways as you can think of how much you care, but if you fail to take the time to caress them and say **"I LOVE YOU"**, sooner or later you come to understand that these three words mean as much as anything you could ever do in a lifetime!

#7

The lack of direction or definitive goals. This combined with a lack of a vision and a philosophy of life that no real power results in improper focus or misdirected energy. We worry about **all the wrong things** or things of **little significance**. In relationships, the focus should be on the individuals doing what's right and checking for feedback. You can only control your thoughts and behavior. If you are not being treated fairly you must decide to get out. This involves some serious pain, but it may be the lesser of two evils. "cut your losses" says Gail Williams. Change your philosophy, you change your energy direction, change your energy direction you change your behavior, change your behavior your life takes a new direction.

#8

SPIRIT KILLERS- The most destructive of the things that are unknown. Black men, in particular, know when they have done wrong because deep down inside we know how good Black women are to us. Therefore, in times of reconciliation for wrong doing, we ride an emotional roller coaster because of what we have been taught. Many times we may have come to grips with our actions and decide to make amends for what we've done and change or improve our behavior. It may come on the way home from work, as we go through the guilt process searching for the right way or an effective way to deal with the situation, there begins to surface a new spirit for living. Quite naturally, our woman has no way of knowing our mental or emotional state, but in many cases one of the issues I previously spoke of will show its head, out of nowhere, comes confrontation and turmoil, leaving the Black man saying what's the use. Take the time to find out what's going in the moment before you attempt to discuss problems or areas of concern, the time may not be right.

#9

The impact of employment on our relationships. It has been estimated that more than one-half of the working population is unhappy with their job situation. Spending eight hours in a situation where you are unhappy, usually the first part of your day, will tend to carry over into your leisure hours. Another spirit killer. Understanding why our situation or environment is the way it is can only lead to the proper solution. Once the understanding comes into being we must accept the change necessary to create the situation or environment we want, deserve, and desire. The final step being taking constant and decisive action to bring about change. It's been said that Nothing comes from doing nothing. Both meanings apply here!

#10

WE HAVE NOT MADE LISTENING A HABIT IN OUR RELATIONSHIPS

1) We must form the habit of listening to what the person **is** saying,

2) refrain from immediately responding to what a person has said **until** we are absolutely certain we known exactly what it is the person really means,

3) ask questions for clarification if we feel hurt by something that is said to us, many times we allow ourselves to be hurt simply because we jumped to the wrong conclusion or misunderstood what a person really meant, Note: If we learn to ask questions that command a real solution, we will begin to receive answers that provide real solutions that work. For example, if you simply ask a Black man, why he won't communicate with you, it will more often than not lead to a very defensive response beginning with "because" of this or that. I don't think the CAUSE is of concern, however, what is of concern is how he feels about you or whatever it is you want him to respond to, not why he won't respond. It is noteworthy to say that Black men must feel this experience of intimacy will only increase the love and respect from his Black Angel before he will be open to the idea.

4) once you think you understand the other persons position, take the time to think through your response, engage your mind before your mouth, remember it is your relationship and if it's worth anything to you this should be easy and well worth the effort.

SECTION 5:

20 COMPELLING QUESTIONS TO ASK BEFORE YOU SAY YES TO A RELATIONSHIP OR MARRIAGE!

INSTRUCTIONS FOR USING THIS GUIDE

Each of the following questions is designed to assist you in making good choices for individuals you deem to be compatible with you and fulfill your needs in a relationship, whether it be marriage or that special someone. This guide is designed to be used over a period of twenty one (21) days. When you are ready to begin, read each question carefully, do not attempt to answer any of the questions, then put them aside until bedtime. Each night before you go to bed, read the question for the next day five times out loud then retire for the evening, this will allow you to sleep on it. The following day spend at **least** thirty (30) minutes to develop your answers for the questions. This guide will cause you to focus on some issues that must be dealt with sooner or later, so why not do it before you commit to a relationship. On the twenty-first (21st) day, examine your answers with this question in mind, "based on what I have indicated in my answers to this guide, what are my chances of success in this relationship?" You'll find that by focusing and dealing with certain issues, you will be able to detect problem areas, thus spend more time being happy! **GOOD LUCK!**

1.   Do you think your prospective lover will change into the person you want him to be once you get married or become intimate?

2.   What is your perception of how married life will be like? Describe a typical week day.

3.   Where do you see yourself and your lover/spouse in 6 months, 1 year, 5 years,.........What goals will you have accomplished?

4.   What value do you place on material things compared to your lover? Have you developed any expectations that have not been openly discussed or revealed? i.e. Is the man expected to pay all the bills? Is the woman expected to do all of the household chores? What items would either of you purchase that would be deemed a waste of money by the other?

5.   When you find yourself in disagreement with your lover once you are married or intimate, who will make the final decision? Will both people be able to support fully the decision that is made? i.e. investments, vacations, the kind of car to purchase, entertainment, etc.

6.   What bad habits does your lover have now that you think you will be able to tolerate once you are married or become very intimate? i.e. making smart remarks,

popping gum, etc. Note: if some little things somewhat bother you now, multiply it by 500 or 600 times, because as time goes on that's exactly how it will seem!

7. What do you and your prospective lover plan to do during your quality time together to maintain that special feeling you now share?

8. What goals have you established together and do they meet the needs of **both** people?

9. How will you divide up the responsibility for maintaining the home: i.e. paying bills, cleaning, cooking, hiring service contractors, car repairs, etc.

10. Will you have the **desire** to fulfill each other's sexual fantasies and do you have the same or similar attitudes about the importance of sex in the marriage or relationship?

11. Has your lover ever displayed any behavior that has embarrassed you in public or with friends?

12. How will problems be resolved so they don't continue to grow?

13. When the chips are down, will your prospective spouse be there for you? Or will you have to find them and drag them back to deal with the problem?

14. Does your prospective lover respect you? How do you know?

15. What would you not be willing to do to make the marriage **or** relationship work? i.e. convert to the other's religion, accept the commitment of your lover to their profession, etc.

16. What would you be willing to do to make the marriage work? i.e. participate in using this guide?????????, let go of the pain from past relationships and start with an atmosphere of trust and respect.

17. What things really infuriate your lover to the point where they may become verbally abusive toward you? (i.e. money, drugs, alcohol, other women, etc.) Knowing the areas identified above, how do you plan to remove these elements from the marriage so this negative environment is not created?

18. What influence will parents have in your marriage or relationship? How will vacations be divided with respect to families? Will family members want to come and live with you? Is it understood that you are expected to

welcome them at any time? How will holidays be divided?

19. Do you have the same attitude about children? How many do you want? How many does he want? Who will be responsible for disciplinary measures?

20. List all the areas you and your prospective lover have in common. List all the areas where you are in complete disagreement. Which list is longer? What areas are non-negotiable?

CONCLUSION

As you may have noticed, I have constantly referred to the Black woman as an Angel. I have done so over and over again in hopes that if you see it enough times, then you will start to believe it.

A self-image or vision less than this does not do Black women justice. When a Black woman feels this way about herself, attracting a Black man into intimacy is a done deal. She has greatness in her being. That is why all men that rise to great levels of success have a very positive Black woman in their past. Believing Black women are truly God's Angels, will begin to change your life in a very positive way. Black women owe it to themselves to feel this way and Black men owe it to themselves to see Black women in this light. The future of the Black family is literally in the control of the Black woman. Our Angels should not forget the tremendous responsibility they have as leader of the wonders of the world, our children, our future. We should model ourselves after these precious creatures, they accept their position in life without question.

God has created this life we live in with such delicate balance that when everything is moving in the same direction, in unison, incredible things will happen. How powerful is a hurricane when all the winds forces are moving in the same direction, in unison, together?

Black men and their Angels, when in unison, moving in the same direction, working together are capable of absolutely astounding achievements, faster than you could ever imagine. Yesterday is gone, unchangeable, but today we can make our dreams come true. It is your life, it is your choice, it is your dream.

AS YOU DEPART FOR YOUR JOURNEY TOWARD TRUE INTIMACY:

When two people have a burning desire to have a successful relationship, they are committed to doing the things that are necessary to make it happen. You have been given a road map to guide you in this direction, as long as you take positive steps each day in that direction you will arrive. We must learn how to hear the words spoken from the one we love with our hearts. We must feel what they say and be committed to unconditional respect. We all must continually strive to express the way we feel in order to reach a much deeper level of understanding. Many times we will have to reword, rephrase, rethink, redo, and undo many of our ways and that takes patience, but for what it's worth, when all is said and done-nothing, I mean, nothing is truly worth losing the love and devotion of someone you truly love.

www.ingramcontent.com/pod-product-compliance
Lightning Source LLC
Chambersburg PA
CBHW071339290326
41933CB00040B/1748